Table of

Part I: Spring time & Childhood 3
    Ruggles Paternal Family Tree 8
    Poems from Childhood 9
        For Love of One Nasty Cat 9
        Tumbleweed 12
        Like Father, Like Daughter 13
        Don't ever let 'em break you, Orie 15
        Becoming an Artist 17
        First Fatality 18

Part II: Summertime: Introduction to Occupational Therapy as Reconstruction Aide and Pioneer 20
    Timeline 26
    Poems on Being Called 27
        Teacher 27
        Fort McPherson September 7, 1918 30
        Reconstruction as the Great Experiment 31
        Epiphany of limbless warriors 33
        Paul – First Meeting 35
        Mosaic 37
        Dixie Café 39
        The day it rained 40
        See Beyond What is Not 42
        Sanctitude 44

Love, Paul 45

Part III: Autumn and Seasoned Therapist 47

    Poems from The Front 55

        Poem for Oscar 55

        The Beauty of the Ordinary 57

        The importance of the ordinary 58

        Nothing sustains me more potently than the poetry of the commonplace 59

        Court Martial 60

        Discharge 62

Part IV: Winter: A Time of Reflection 64

    Poems from Reflection and Retirement 74

        Routine: All that remains 74

        Old 75

        Role 76

        Habitual 77

        Rituals 79

Part I: Spring time & Childhood

Ora Ruggles, one of the first reconstruction aides and arguably *the* pioneer of Occupational Therapy, was born on the 16th day of April in 1894. She was the youngest of five children, born with a mop of flaming red curls. Originally from Appalachia, her family migrated west and she was born in a cabin made of mud and logs on a ranch in Western Nebraska. Thomas and Nancy Ruggles had five children in a 12 year span – Laura, two years later Art, then two years later Pearl, four years later Merle and finally, four more years later Ora was born. She was the beloved, welcome and secure baby of a large, loving brood and always remained the 'pet' of the family.

Nancy Ann Ruggles nee Osborn was 40 when Ora was born, a small woman, about 5 feet tall and said to have weighed about 100 pounds. She had red hair, dark eyes and kept a serene rhythm in the day-to-day life tasks: Mothering, baking bread, butchering, putting up preserves, tending sick cattle, and nurturing both hired hands and a family of seven. She was fearless, certain that harm could not come to one who believed in God, told the truth and followed a strict code of right and wrong. When Ora was 3 years old, two haggard Indians came to the cabin, peered in and called to Nancy, "Beeskit, beeskit! (bread, bread!)". Nancy, unflapped, greeting them with tempered compassion and a loaded rifle for caution, went to see what they wanted. Seeing they were more to be pitied than feared, she invited them in, fed them and sent them along with sandwiches for their trip. Turning to her children she said, "Never get scared until you know what there is to be scared about. It's usually nothing."

Thomas Jacob Ruggles could not have been more different than his wife. Thomas, Tom, was 48 when Ora was born. He was considered one of the strongest men in Nebraska, sported a rollicking love of life and he was willing to prove his pluck to any who challenged him. He was well over six feet tall, dark haired with grey eyes, and sported a ruddy complexion. He had a bull-like neck that was covered by a spade beard, weighed 200 pounds and was intolerant of a collar or tie. Said to be hearty and handsome, hot-headed, aggressive, seldom serious, unfailingly optimistic, fast-talking, and adventurous, he was a man known for his glib-tongued charm. He used flattery, jokes, tall tales and outright cunning to best others in horse trading and earned warm admiration across Nebraska. He had a deeply tender, caring side which he revealed only to those closest to him; this he passed on to Ora.

The family had 5 children: Laura was the oldest, with black hair and soft brown eyes. She was said to have a strange sense of refined detachment about her. Perhaps related, she became deaf at the age of 12 when she was attacked by a severe case of Whooping Cough. Laura was like a second mother to Ora. Two years younger than Laura was a brother, Art. He was a stereotypical ranch boy, lanky, red-headed, an unrepentant teaser, and full of piss and vinegar. He was Ora's first teacher and taught her to wrestle, ride horses, play baseball, shoot, hunt rabbit and kill a snake without flinching. Two years younger than Art, Pearl bounced between being a brown-haired, dark-eyed, girly girl, and a rough-and-tumble tomboy. The battle continued until, at the age of 12, Pearl finally decided between the hoyden-like wildness of her sister Ora and the lady-like decorum of her mother and sister Laura; she opted to become a lady. Merle was 4 years younger than Pearl and 4 years older than Ora and had, for those first eight years, appointed herself to be the boss of Ora. Practically twins, both Merle and Ora sported mops of flaming curls but at last, Ora overpowered Merle when she found the consummate outflanking move: One frog dangled within 6 inches of Merle's face and any battle was decidedly Ora's.

    Thomas Ruggles' best friend and family doctor was Doctor Duncan, Doc Duncan. Doc was recognized as the best doctor in Western Nebraska who reached not just for the hands of his patients but deep inside them, somehow, as if to shake any infirmity from their very hearts. Nancy suffered him as a 'necessary evil', a man who cursed, drank, and used an uncanny gruffness with patients to shake life and health back into them. Ora saw that Doc, like her own father's well-kept secret, had a deep sensitivity and unyielding compassion for his patients. While Nancy 'suffered' Doc as a necessary evil, Ora came to love and admire him deeply. One bitter winter, after recovering from pneumonia, four-year-old Ora drew a goatee on her chin using soot from the stove, strutted throughout the house and barked at her mother, "When the hell am I gonna get out this goddam house?" That was the last time Ora cursed in front of her mother, reserving her newly discovered habits of spitting, cursing, and growling to times she spent with her father, Doc Duncan, hired hands on the ranch and visiting horse buyers.

When Ora was 5, the Ruggles family moved to a 640 acre ranch. These sodbusters thrived on the openness of prairie life, loved the poetry and power of the countryside and raised prosperity from the somewhat primitive rolling plains. Harvest and roundup were exciting times, as the Ruggleses welcomed 30 hired hands and neighbors to help. Ora flourished in the habits and rituals of a strong, loving, loyal community. She was a product of this geography – the tension of opposition, the pace of life ordered by the unpredictable demands of nature and community, the richness of living within a community of unfailing compassion and care. Her father told her:

> "No one ever really dies. All living things, when they've spent their span of years, leave something behind them – a seed, an influence, a memory, call it what you like. It all contributes to a greater life. People, well, they're like a great procession, steadily marching forward. Individuals drop out but the parade goes on, getting mightier by the minute. It's a miraculous thing, Ora. Pretty soon I'll drop out of the procession, but I won't really be gone. I'll be marching right along with you. You're me. I'll always be with you." (Carlova & Ruggles, p. 28)

Around 60 years of age, Tom was diagnosed with diabetes. His family didn't know until 3 years later when he collapsed and Doc Duncan delivered the news to the family. Tom died when he was 64 years old. Following his directions, the Ruggles family sold the ranch and moved to California to be near Nancy's sister. Ora, then 15, entered high school and pursued her passion for art.

The partial family tree on the next page shows that Ora's ancestor James Ruggles emigrated from England. Following that the chart shows a steady movement westward, which perhaps hints at the Ruggles family spirit of pioneering and independence.

Ruggles Paternal Family Tree

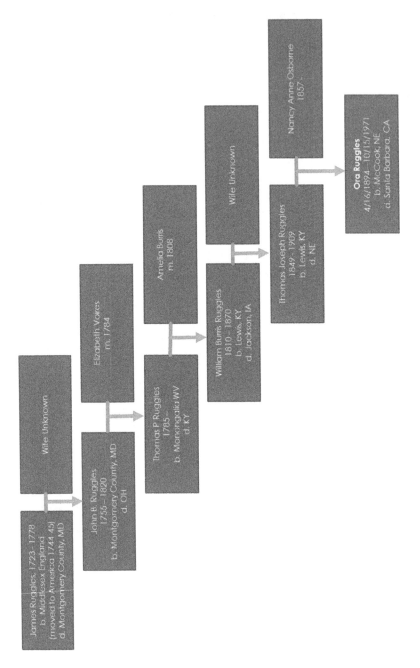

Poems from Childhood

For Love of One Nasty Cat

Tough minded

Felt mercy only for those who showed mettle through their persistence,

who had to overcome invisible chasms and emerged courageous.

Ora grew centered when around those who had traversed a chasm,

The ones who seemed lost to grief and living still, defiantly, clutching a last ember of life.

She was an odd child, none questioned,

at peace in the center of what appeared, to others, as opposition.

Mother dressed her each morning in well-sewn dresses,

carefully plaited, ribbon-tied pigtails but Ora, a girl more adept with a rifle,

a pitchfork, a bridle and cursing with the hired hands than

lavender scented soap or expertly kneaded bread of her mother's tidy kitchen.

She liked the muck, found peace in that purposeful work. Instead of bread,

Ora set out rows and rows of copperheads and rattlers she had beheaded, or the rarer prize

A bested Timber Rattler.

Mother, in one desperately hopeful gesture, gave Ora a doll,

almost as tall as a child itself, dressed so perfectly as a miniature Ora

> – bloomers, gingham, braids neatly plaited and adorned with optimistic ribbon.

The doll seemed to be loved, at first, Ora tended to it, offered her sips of warm cream

during the morning milking. After one day, that doll was found, naked, discarded in haphazardly

piled mounds of unruly rancid hay. The doll's pantaloons and dress

used to clothe the one-eyed insufferable, barn cat, the one who wore the scars of many almost-

lost battles, who pissed and hissed at all of them, that nasty cat,

And why you may wonder and W*hy?* her mother asked? Ora's answer --

> Because, *he breathes and needed them more.* No other words were offered.

That day Ora exposed her center, truth of nature, purpose if one were to look back

That day Ora first reached for then touched more than wound, a heart encrusted in muck

Purpled by suffocation, mettled, persistent, nevertheless,

both protected as well as trapped beneath a boney cage, gnawed raw

made fragile by past trauma

Ora wanted, no needed to have more to offer than pity and to the cat,

that nasty cat

she offered the gingham, the bloomers, and the bows.

Something split opened that day, she bowed to the sanctity of breath and something

Some fate, entered, a breath for even the least amongst us,

the nastiest of cats, entered. Ora was ever after followed by the infirm, the crippled,

the disreputable

> Three-footed collie, his paw ripped clean off by the coyote,
>
> The horse born dyspraxic and mean spirited
>
> The sow who whined and whined unless given shade.

And the cat

> That one-eyed nasty cat
>
> Who began crying out for a touch or a scratch on the ear,
>
> But only from her.

Tumbleweed

Like her father, she understood both horses and men
    Able to subdue a wild-eyed mustang at 8
    Able to out-spit or out-haggle horse traders
She never walked
    when she could run
    Never acted like a lady should
Noisily she moved in and out of spaces
    A tornado of a girl
    like the Nebraskan prairie
        Wild and free
        Naturally alive
They say, she found a slice of calm, at last,
When she discovered she had a talent for drawing.
    She sketched buffalo and tumbleweed
    Caricatures of schoolmates.

They say she yearned to explore life to its fullest, yes, those very words
    That she yearned to discover
    How a woman could be useful
    Beyond accepted roles
        mother, wife, cook.

Like Father, Like Daughter

> The Ruggles family settled in Morgantown West Virginia, then moved to Kentucky where Tom was born in 1849. Tom married and took his wife first to Iowa, and then, by wagon train he and Nancy settled their own lives in Nebraska.

Tom Ruggles

Dark-haired, grey eyed, adventurous Appalachian man,

At times het up, hearty as he was handsome.

He loved the vast openness of land, loved the sodbuster life,

Prairie life seemed to suit him, the primitive, magnificent, rolling green plains,

The rippling buffalo grass

No trees to speak of but in the gullies, near Red Willow Creek

Scrubs and saplings reached toward the infinity of the open sky,

Adorned by grape vines entwined and fruit heavy in their adolescent branches.

Ora Ruggles

Almost as tall as her father, strong, a temper to match his own

She too was enthralled by both poetry and the promise of this prairie landscape

The powerfulness of an unending topography.

She, her father, the land

Could each be peaceful or restless

    Brutal or gentle

        Blazing or frigid

Sometimes calm, like heaven

    Other times black, fuming, Stormed.

The prairie was wild, free, "Like us, like me" she once said.

Ora, the youngest of his children, his pet,

Was, like her father entranced by the riotousness of the corrals,

Willing to show her prowess if challenged

Thought no job too tough or boyish, for slim-hipped, gingham-dressed Ora.

At seven, she could cut a cow out of a herd.

At eight, she could rope and subdue a wild-eyed mustang and terrorize her sister

With a quickly produced frog.

If in danger, her father was always there to protect her,

It was he, Tom, who taught her that the big and strong must look after the weak.

Still, if she erred, he was there to correct

A wallop on her behind was his way and the way of those times, and with that

he taught her how compassion and strength often go hand in hand.

Tom bequeathed Ora both his temper and his rollicking love of life.

Don't ever let 'em break you, Orie

Doc Duncan, the first warrior Ora knew,

was merciless

A rare soldier who fought diseases, witlessness, and often defended

the line between life and death for the people in the small Nebraska town.

Doc was observably hardened by life, his face creviced like baked earth

cracked and stippled from too much whiskey and loss.

Doc Duncan never lost his spirit. In fact, it seemed to grow each time drawn upon -- a secret weapon

Ora begged him to reveal.

He was, to Ora, beloved, an indomitable old warrior,

He saw, in Ora, something special, the smoldering pre-sparks of warrior stock.

It was Doc, who armed her with what he knew of medicine, and resolve.

Ora watched this skeletal warrior, learned to grow her own strength,

learned how to exterminate dispassion's seed.

Doc Duncan taught Ora to square her broad shoulder and heave

against the force of despair

with her own interminable force of life.

When death came to the door of her own home, the reaper casting about for her own father, it was Doc Duncan who came, bequeathed Ora with the shield she would carry with her,

for a lifetime in battle. Doc Duncan said, and said it softly,

Don't ever let 'em break you, Orie, Don't ever let 'em break you.

Aspiration

    To be an artist

        To be true to something inside of her

            Calling her to something

                No one could name.

Saw

    Lew, her first man-crush

        Lost his son then his wife

            Then his dream

                    Retreated, free and unhampered to the prairie

                Some small sad victory

He told her

    It's a hard row to hoe

        Especially for a gal

            In the early 1900's.

                Be a teacher, he said,

                    Go along, but

                            go along with yourself too and
                            your dream

First Fatality

Tom Ruggles 1849 - 1909

I.

In 1908,

Ora's childhood ended.

No longer able to withhold the news

Doc Duncan dispensed bitter news to the Ruggles family

Standing in birth order by their father's bedside

Tom lay still, broken, ashamed that he had collapsed and been carried home by his wife and put in bed,

shrunken into shadow.

Laura, Pearl and Merle stood on his left, alongside of mother.

Art with Ora flanked the right. Doc looked directly at Ora, the youngest of the issue,

And said, *Be strong --*

> *It's time you knew -- There is nothing more I can do*
>
> *Your father's sugar diabetes is a death sentence*
>
> *He will be gone from you by the spring.*

Tom was 48 when Ora was born.

died when she turned 15. He bequeathed each child what they needed but for Ora, he

Insisted, before his last breath, that Ora move to California and realize her dream of school and of art.

II

Ora traveled west until there was no more land

She enrolled at Manual Arts High School and learned to paint, to draw and to sculpt.

She studied interior design, woodwork and furniture making.

She played tennis, basketball

Was voted most popular girl in the school

Won a beauty contest.

1912 Ora, while attending San Diego Normal where one trains to be a teacher,

She studied an exciting, emerging field Psychology

She pushed against petty rules and regulations she was entranced by the meeting with

an intense young socialist, Upton Sinclair.

1914, she turned 20, the war had broken and Ora

Longing to be of use,

First became an artist of patriotic propaganda, art well received and used across the US.

Successful, her art began to sell – jewelry, sculptures, paintings, she even constructed model chairs

But all the while she pursued her art,

In spite of her best intentions

her teaching, solid and tradition,

brought in the livable wage.

Part II: Summertime: Introduction to Occupational Therapy as Reconstruction Aide and Pioneer

> "Take the human body. What is it but a frail sack of fluids and bones? It's not surprising when it's punctured or demolished, especially on the battlefield. But take the human spirit. That can't be demolished, not even when the body is despoiled or destroyed."
>
> -Paul Remland   p 45

Ora graduated with a degree in teaching Manual Arts. She developed a reputation for being able to hold her own against rough-neck, reluctant learners. But in 1916-1917, news of horror came to where she was teaching, in California, including photos of broken and battered men littering battlefields in Europe. Eventually an invitation arose to engage in a daring experiment of reconstruction; to create the means of recovery through pleasurable occupations. Ora found the call irresistible.

On September 7, 1918, Ora Ruggles arrived at Fort McPherson Army Base on the southwest edge of Atlanta, Georgia. Ora, 24 years old, was greeted by a very craggy Captain Harrington, and the wounded warriors, men with heads bandaged, trouser-legs pinned up where a leg once was, signs of madness, of bitterness, of barely suppressed rage, and worst of all, the blankness of deadened spirits. Over 5000 cases of human devastation represented the wreckage from World War I. She was there to help by providing occupations to divert their minds from misfortune. More than this, her goal was to make them aware of life and to want life, and to enable them to respond to the call of a new future. From Captain Harrington, she met doubt, hostility and the verdict that "girls like you shouldn't be working at an army hospital." From the wounded, her figure and titian hair garnered cat-calls. She bunked in the nurse's quarters, where it was quickly made clear to her that she was not welcome. She must have asked herself what she was doing there. She steeled herself with her mother's words, "Never get scared until you know what there is to be scared about." She was shielded, always, by the armor bequeathed to her by the indomitable old warrior Doc Duncan, "Don't let 'em break you, Orie". She stood steady, she rallied, she stayed. Ora was unlike the reconstruction aides who had come, and left, before her.

Once on the hospital floor, she was resolute, made the most of her attributes, used all that she was for a therapeutic presence. She was invited to dance by a man with no legs, his taunt followed by another soldier who said, 'he won't step on your feet, lady, he ain't got no feet!" She allowed and embraced the gruesome humor, toughened by those many moments of spitting and cursing on the ranch.

It was that day she met Paul, the only man she would ever love, taller than she, his manner gallant, sardonic and a little sad. Paul explained to her that the army, the nurses and doctors all, had concluded reconstruction aides were meddlesome, untrained interlopers and that the ward full of ghastly armless, legless, dangerous apparitions was no place for 'nice young ladies.' Before the war, he had been a concert pianist. After the war, he was an officer – a wounded warrior who had lost two fingers on his right hand. He proved to be Ora's equal.

Ora had to overcome many barriers – the Army physicians, nurses and perhaps the patients themselves had not yet learned the value of Reconstruction Aides. The nurses she bunked with were 'hardened old hands who had their feelings trained out of them' and who were unrepentantly resentful. Ora met the Army on its own ground and fought to make a space for herself, and eventually for other Reconstruction Aides, with sodbuster grit. She was known for physically defending her space as well as using her horse-trading wit. She was Tom's daughter, never known to back down from a fight, Nancy's daughter, never one to be afraid of anything before she understood, and Doc Duncan's protégé, never willing to let others grind her down. Once, she arranged to have all the nurse's underwear heavily starched, a move that enabled Ora and the other Reconstruction Aides (almost 50 now) to get to the inadequate bathing facilities first where she enjoyed a long, hot-water hogging indulgent, uncrowded shower. She learned to navigate the Army's red-tape to obtain supplies for the interventions and occupations she felt were needed by the men. Drawing on her past role of teacher and artist, Ora prescribed basket weaving to limber fingers and ordered reeds and equipment to start the work.

> "The human body is a wonderful machine, even when parts are missing. Most people have resources and reserves they don't know about. My job, as I see it, is to bring out those resources and reserves in handicapped patients." (Carlova & Ruggles, p. 52)

She won over the men with her courage, compassion and her unique ability to touch their hearts. She won over the Army with her conniving and her success in supporting limbless warriors to feel whole and enabled. She won Paul's heart with her beauty and her fighter's spirit. She found 'crying corners", hidden places in hospitals where she could release the overwhelming feelings she absorbed each day, both overwhelming joys and unbearable grief.

Meanwhile, others across the US were discovering how to use occupation as a therapeutic intervention to help people return to productive, fulfilling lives. Susan Tracy was training nurses at Adams-Nervine and published her lectures, which Ora read. She read the books published by Dr. William Rush Dunton in 1915 documenting his work at Sheppard and Pratt hospital in Towson MD. She followed the work of Dr. Herbert Hall of Marblehead Massachusetts who prescribed occupations for the patients with mental health concerns. As this work was underway across the United States, George Barton, an architect and engineer, and a man who had suffered TB, amputation and hysterical paralysis (known now as Conversion disorder), organized pioneers in occupational therapy. Dr. Dunton, Susan Johnson (a nurse and professor at Columbia University), Thomas Kidner, and Eleanor Clarke Slagle, a social worker, were present in 1917 to form the Society for the Promotion of Occupational Therapy, later known as AOTA. Slagle sought Ora out, met her and invited her to share her ongoing discoveries, to shout to one another and shout loud in order to make medical history and grow the knowledge base of the profession. Ora and the Reconstruction Aides at Fort McPherson reported faithfully on their discoveries. Ora's most profound discovery, one might argue, was that as she improved, her patients improved, as she grew concerned, wanted wellness for the man, he wanted wellness. The discovery was 'It's not enough to give a patient something to do with his hands. You must reach for the heart as well as the hands. It's the heart that really does the healing." (Carlova & Ruggles, p. 69)

    Ora and her fellow Reconstruction Aides recognized early that challenging exercise that produced something of beauty and worth, helped patients discover unexpected inner resources. One occupation used in the wards, knitting, calmed the mind and damped down the inevitable anxiety the soldiers felt. The needles clicked, hand coordination improved and many scarves were produced. Rake knitting and looming were introduced, and eventually thousands of women – wives and mothers and girlfriends of wounded warriors – began to receive and wear fantastic lengths of bright-red knitwear. In almost any American city in 1918, women were seen dragging bright red trailing trains, warm reminders of men they loved healing through occupation. Traditional gender lines were being erased – women engaged in crafts previously viewed to be 'men's work' and men were learning lace work and needlework. Occupational therapy became a subversive act in part as an expression of Ora Ruggles's unflinching, unapologetic zeal for full-out engagement regardless of expectations from traditionalists. She began to follow Dr. Richard Cabot's work who said men live by four things: work, play, love and worship. She would read Dr. Cabot's writings to the soldiers and say *"You have the spiritual strength of a human being. Let me help you use it."* (*Carlova & Ruggles, p.* 75) Ora saw not what was missing but what remained. The ward was a place of quiet industry but not without shrapnel.

Ora learned, the day it rained, that war was hell. Ora lost Paul who died, eventually from the shrapnel shards that had invaded his lungs. Ora lost her ability to buoy herself up over the tragedy Fort McPherson reminded her of and after Paul's death, after having been at Fort McPherson for a little over a year, she was given a train ticket and ordered home, to California, feeling old and tired and haggard.

The timeline on the following page attempts to place Ora's lifetime into historical context. On the timeline, one can see the major wars; the life-spans of other prominent figures of OT; and a selection of notable cultural, technological, and historical events.

Timeline

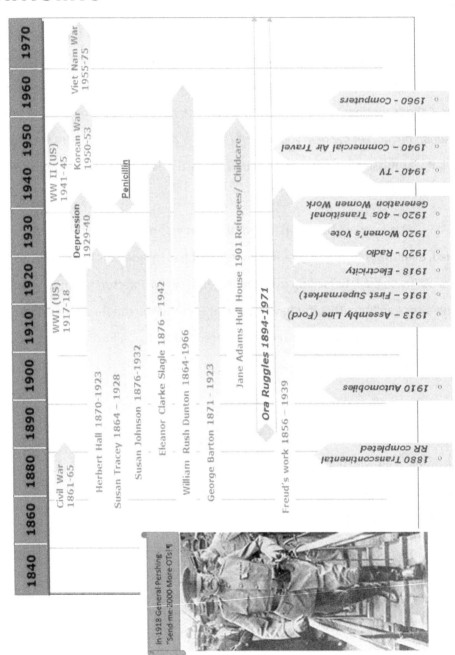

Timeline entries (1840–1970):

- Civil War 1861-65
- Herbert Hall 1870-1923
- Susan Tracey 1864 – 1928
- Susan Johnson 1876-1932
- Eleanor Clarke Slagle 1876 – 1942
- William Rush Dunton 1864-1966
- George Barton 1871 - 1923
- Jane Adams Hull House 1901 Refugees/ Childcare
- Ora Ruggles 1894-1971
- Freud's work 1856 – 1939
- WWI (US) 1917-18
- WW II (US) 1941-45
- Korean War 1950-53
- Viet Nam War 1955-75
- Depression 1929-40
- Penicillin

- 1880 Transcontinental RR completed
- 1910 Automobiles
- 1913 – Assembly Line (Ford)
- 1916 – First Supermarket
- 1918 – Electricity
- 1920 – Radio
- 1920 Women's Vote
- 1920 – 40s Transitional Generation Women Work
- 1940 - TV
- 1940 – Commercial Air Travel
- 1960 - Computers

In 1918 General Pershing "Send me 2000 More OTs!"

Poems on Being Called

Teacher

> Ora, after all her years at College, appeared before the full faculty to face expulsion. In spite of her many years of study, she was to be denied a teaching certificate and instead, given instant dismissal because, during her first day as a teacher-in-training, she had committed a serious offense: She hit a student. Her mentor Dr. Bliss, intervened for Ora and she graduated but he knew just where she should start her teaching career. The challenge was irresistible.

Day one

Substitute teacher in the Manual Training class, woodshop one might say today. A classroom filled only with boys, they judged her female and as such, unworthy.
They heckled her. Unable to deter her, one boy, emblazed, slammed a plank down on his workbench to teach her who was boss. Pitilessly, without hesitation, as if encountering a gauntlet tossed before her or a stallion in need of taming, a rattler perhaps, Ora, unwilling to be schooled, marched toward the boy, seized him, bent him like she would a soon-to-be-branded calf and sure enough whacked his rear with the same plank he had dared to slam on the table minutes before.

At last, he surrendered, ran screaming from the classroom. His terror summoned the principle, who in turn dismissed her for the day. The following day, Ora, stood, unrepentant, before the full faculty of San Diego Normal, was told she had forfeited her right to earn her degree, faced instant dismissal.

Day two

Her unrepentant defense when called before the full faculty was to justify the essential need for a teacher to maintain order, to show strength in the face of battle, a lesson from her father, mother, mentors all, never back down. After deliberation, and only because her mentor persevered, she was,
at last, provided one option for salvation. Ora was to graduate and accepted dispatch to El Centro, to teach the toughest crowd of roughnecks in all of California.
She earned a reputation for holding steady in the face of roughnecks. Still, no one seemed to want this temperamental teacher, gifted though she seemed to be in the manual arts.
Dr. Bliss, mentor, visionary, champion for education, knew who needed a warrior, knew where to dispatch one who could yield compassion with the same fierceness as she could open hearts.
Ora was sent to reconstruct learning at an underperforming school in Imperial Valley.

Day three

Standing before the class of ruffians, Ora was fended off the unwelcoming shower
4-foot long arrow weeds shaved into lethal weapons
Launched toward her by 60 shaggy-headed, unruly students.
She rounded up both arrow weeds and children as best she could
Faced the rising din of children, ages ranging from 6 to 15
Until, at last, the children shouted at her and began to dance, a war dance to be sure
Hoping to make short order of this so-called teacher. But what they could not have known
They had met a warrior like none other, one who could out run and behead a copper, best the wildest buck and wrestle any man to the mat. The dance, the shouting, the opposition continued until, at last, Ora, red-faced, temper frayed, brandished a baseball bat against the unruly. She lashed the legs of one boy with the very arrow weed he had dared to throw, she chased him out along with any others who dared to challenge her.

Then the parents came, and you knew they would, pinch-faced and hard. Ora met them, without a flinch, forced them to look in the mirror she held up to them: this dilapidated school, a jungle for a play yard, beastly hooligans instead of willing learners.She told them the truth: they bore the title of 'worst school' in the state, asked, *Do I stay on my terms, or go, as the other 3 teachers have?"*

End of the year, 1916

Her good hard sense won them over. Horse-trader, warrior, upholder of even the ugly truths,
Together they painted the school, built a playground and constructed an environment that enabled
learning. She played baseball with the older boys, taught all the children to love reading, inspired with
her infectious enthusiasm for life. It was exhausting to properly teach, to convert beasts back to
children.

Promoted, perhaps a repreived, she taught next at a more friendly school.
But the world was changing, challenges beyond the classroom tom-foolery pulled at her heart
And a new call took her to Atlanta.

Fort McPherson September 7, 1918

Burning heat clung to the ground like a dense fog of burning sulfur

Beyond the smoky half-light strange incomplete figures stood like wraiths

Creatures of purgatory, trapped in various stages of transformation to the invisible

Khaki shirtsleeves hung limp, empty, trouser-legs pinned up out of the way

where flesh should be

Nothing.

Lucky ones showed a dulled bitterness in their set lips, felt a.

Rage, barely suppressed, burning their red rimmed eyes ;

those, without spirit, the most battered of all, stood dazed or sat legless in wheeled wicker chairs.

Ora was pressed by the human devastation around her

One woman in the center of the fort,

Surrounded by hundreds of silenced, war-ravaged soldiers.

She straightened to her full 5'10" frame, removed the hat from her fire-red curls, and turned to the

Captain who greeted her with an unbridled lack of enthusiasm

Said "I've more than pity to offer these men" and marched to her bunk determined

To teach occupations and make five thousand men aware of a life they could want again.

> "The absence of occupation is not rest; a mind quite vacant is a mind distressed." Dr. Benjamin Rush

Spring 1909, after her father died, Ora moved to California

enrolled at Manual Arts High School

Learned to paint and to draw

Sculpted, studied interior design, woodwork and furniture making.

She played tennis, basketball

Was voted most popular girl in the school

Won a beauty contest.

1912 Ora attended San Diego Normal

A teaching school. Studied the new field of psychology

Began to push aside petty rules and regulations and

Met the intense young socialist Upton Sinclair.

1914, when twenty, Ora volunteered her services

An artist of patriotic propaganda used across the US

She began to sell her art – jewelry, sculptures, paintings constructed

Model chairs but teaching brought her income.

In her first teaching job she was dismissed for hitting a surly student

unrepentant, her reputation for holding steady in the face of roughnecks earned her a challenging position to reconstruct learning in Imperial Valley,

She wielded a baseball bat attempting to bring order to the unruly,

against four-foot-long arrow weeds shaved into lethal weapons. Her good hard sense

turned the hearts of the community. Together they painted the school,

built a playground and constructed an environment that enabled learning.

In 1917, the news of horror came to El Centro,

photos of broken and battered men littering battlefields in Europe.

Invited to engage in a daring experiment of reconstruction, to create the means of recovery through

pleasurable occupations.

Epiphany of limbless warriors

All around her, limbless warriors, swarms of broken men

surrendered, broken, dispirited wounded men who didn't know to hope for more than death.

They could not envision human life could be worth living

if not whole, felt themselves inhuman without both arms, both legs

No one had learned, yet, that a human body, this sad frail sack of fluids and bones was really spirit,

Or that spirit remained, unspoiled, alive, whole

even when the body had been mutilated by battle.

They didn't know until they met Ora, that life remains waiting for breath, inspiration, and purpose.

From warriors, wounded, Ora learned

courage is not enough

having something to do with one's hands, not enough

True fighters, true warriors fight against hopeless odds,

Not enough. She had to find a way to lead them into a new battle, to be enough

a battle for reconstruction

a battle against oppressive despair,

A battle to unveil the spirit that remained.

She said she had to grow a warrior's heart herself to lead the charge

And to do so first, each time, for each of them.

She said she had to have capacity to connect to true tragedy

To want another's well-being more than they could fathom it, to hold that hope until they had the strength

To want it for their own, to have the will to reach and hope for the impossible

Ora said it was there, in the wards at Fort McPherson, that she learned

It wasn't enough to give a task to be completed,

not enough to merely distract,

not enough to engage the hands. She learned, if humanity is to be reunited with spirit, if whole men were to be reconstructed

returned to some inner sanctified sense of home,

one must find the courage to reach for the heart as well as the hands

It was here, in her first year of service, that she learned,

it's the heart that really does the healing.

Paul – First Meeting

"Of course I'm not allowed to take you to breakfast."

I.

It's the relentless fighters who need help more than most

I love them, I do, I admire how they continue

Fighting against hopeless odds.

They seem tough but they are softest beneath the wounds,

and more than any others, they need warmth,

need to be understood by someone who has a capacity for real tragedy

someone who can call out to their spirit, name it by name and demand it show itself, demand it be brave. I love that part of the fighter, the soft part that can never be destroyed and will rise, always, even if gouged and bloody, even one-eyed, carrying a pitiful excuse for what was at one time a splendid shield, I love,

I do, those who stand erect with defiant pluck when courage and strength of the warrior are not enough.

II.

Paul had been a concert pianist before the war

Before his right hand was carved by shrapnel,

Where two middle fingers had once been, one ugly scar

Not bitter, not depressed, Paul stood by Ora, professed his religion

Meaning found in life, clean clothes, silk underwear, tailored uniforms, indulgent long leisurely enjoyed baths, day to day celebration

that he was no longer left to wallow in blood soaked, muddy trenches

He confided he was composing a concerto for eight fingers, for Ora. He confided that he loved her at first sight.

III.

He asked her out on the first day he met her, their first date, breakfast.

He wasn't allowed to do that. She asked if she was allowed to go.

She knew she'd found love when he grinned and countered,

"with all that wonderful red hair, Miss Ora, I wouldn't have taken you as one to make decisions based on what's permitted….

Assuming you can climb through a fence."

Ora saw what was present

Not of life but of *living*

Not just breath

Inspiration

She was moved by spirit, could sense an ember remaining the colorlessness of ash,

She felt mercy for the frightened, cared for the defeated, sure

But she discovered, early, a secret truth in the lives lived by misfits and failures, the fools and rebels

Those who

For all purpose were disrespected

She saw hidden nuggets of god, she saw blazing courage and a willingness to wait

For grace to find them, for those who had enough compassion to believe, beyond hope, there was gold behind festering scars.

Ora believed, as did her father, that there was a great procession of souls moving one another

Invisibly urging each of us, corporal beings, to feel them, to feel their dance, and join in

Ora believed if we have the courage to allow their touch

to reach for their outstretched finger

any flexion in even the most distal digit

if we extend ourselves,

we connect with God.

Ora believed

when her father wasted, diabetes rotting his limbs

when her mother, lopsided from the stroke still cooked and cleaned and encouraged

Ora believed one small effort of her own extension

could orchestrate her entrance to the procession of souls

Life to life abutted,

Bonded with a fired mortar to form a mosaic march

Dixie Café

Well-appointed with one pool table, one battered but well-tuned piano and three weather-beaten, cheerfully profane waitresses, the Dixie Café served Dixie Dew with a side of eggs, bacon, ham, gravy and grits.

Ora taught Paul to weave reeds into baskets
Paul helped Ora strategically outmaneuver regulations and resentment
He grew more nimble-fingered
She more tactical
Ora arranged to have the nurses' underwear washed, heavily starched
She enjoyed her long, hot shower while they were detained.

Paul treated her to dinners at the Dixie Café
To pay her back a little for all she had given to him
And the other men.
Neither of them had much cash
Paul paid for them both with his art, proficient and adept --
He played, 8-fingered, skillfully and with great style.

Ora, an artist in people
Paul, an artist of living life.

The day it rained

"Where there is love for mankind, there is love for the art of healing."
Hippocrates

Shrapnel landed in 65 places and left Richard missing one arm, one leg, bandaged except for his eyes

His terror stricken orbs searched the room for emancipation, the need to let

war ooze out. His lips could barely move, stitched asymmetrically to cover where flesh had once been,

quiet squeaks of woundedness began to escape from tiny swollen tubes when his eye found Ora.

A weapon of words discharged, sound cruelly vibrating across ropes that gave him voice

> *I was buried, a pile of bodies rained on me after the blast, all dead, scraps from a slaughterhouse: a naked thigh, a head with its eyes open, a headless body drowning me*

> *I was drowning from their lifeless weight. God forgive me I scratched through that soggy mass of flesh, desperate for air, clawed until at last a new shell exploded and freed me, tore me loose from the rubble of corpses, scraps of men I knew snored, punned without mercy or pined.*

> *I was hit, baseballs pummeling me again and again until at last I landed in darkness. I woke floating on ground that moved gently, warmth at last. The darkness came again when I realized I was drifting down the trench in a stream of blood.*

It rained today a personal narrative

The story burst like shrapnel from the warrior,

Exposing his shot-up soul

Ora was unprotected

Unshielded to battle.

but she did not flinch when the rain of horror poured and poured and poured

she did not wipe herself clean or turn or run to shield herself from the outpour

Instead

She held Richard's remaining hand, and when he was finished, she stayed,

watched him sleep

Drawing on his strength to restore her own exhausted soul and forever wounded spirit.

In each single drop of water is the essence of the infinite, eternal ocean

All of it, saline, silica, tentacle ink, sailor urine.

The snapped shots of this reflected world,

The ocean's secrets held in bottomlessness and released untranslated in undulation and spray. I thirst.

I drink. I do not think to curse what I miss, the rest of the sea that is

Instead I savor this drop, this wholeness, the good and the bad

Beaten clean against rock

Salve for what was before parched and empty.

In the single man is the essence of humanity

All of it, salvation, saliva, blood, a lover's release.

In his one remaining eye, I see his war, deep, bottomless, terror's unrepentant clench,

I see all of God in the fool who remains, laughing as he falls to the floor

Forgetting again he has left his legs in the blood of battle. We belly laugh in spite of good taste. I wet my

own size 7 panties and laugh harder at my weakness until

I catch a glimpse of that eye.

I guess we all thirst to be loved, to be forgiven, to be quenched in spite of impurities

I drink him in, his one armed, one eyed no-legged-self splashed on the floor

Bringing laughter, reminding us all in his forgetfulness

Not to curse what we miss

To savor what has returned, to enable what can become

He redeems us all with his brazen acceptance of incompleteness.

Sanctitude

I confess to any who do not know this,

hidden in every hospital

Clinic, sanatorium where both anguish and relief

splatter across open halls and corridors

radiate along the sharp edges of mocking sun streaming in

warming selective souls it seems

I admit that hidden in shadowy crooks

I release the overflow of fullness I have known

    accomplishment, wellbeing, new life

Or emptiness I can no longer bear

    Malicious shrapnel, triumphant death angels

I tell Paul, that when I can no longer contain tears by will or physical pain

    The bridge of the nose pinched *hard*

    Increased tonicity in the round muscle of my lid

I seek out Crying Corners

Secreted vestibules

Anterooms where my tears can flow

Freed in the sacredness of

separation.

Love, Paul

The plan unfolded

Paul would teach in Atlanta,

They would marry. He was formally discharged

They were waiting, just, for the periodic surgical probing for shrapnel splinters in his chest.

In the end, it was the shrapnel splinters that migrated to his lungs

And the infection they cultivated there

And then tuberculosis.

He lay in bed

Wasting

One day

It rained

Dark clouds released their burden

Paul told Ora

Because I have loved you, so much,

I will live forever.

The end came calmly, at least

They stood together on that delicate ephemeral place

the life-death threshold, where a touch of the hand, so intimate now, so timeless

in those moments they lived out the lifetime together

denied to them on earth.

Paul

Ora

Both good soldiers but even the best solider has to retreat sometimes. After two years,

After starting a great new movement,

She was given a train ticket home, to California, ordered,

out of love

>*Go home.*

The rain, beaded on the window, echoed back to her broken spirit

Her tired, haggard face.

Part III: Autumn and Seasoned Therapist

When Ora returned to California and her family, she felt empty. Paul's death had ripped a part of her out that she couldn't seem to recover. She began to wear her hair severely drawn back as if to deny her own beauty. She felt an awful hollowness, wretched if she caught herself appreciating beauty. Grief had taken hold of her, serpentine, strangling. Her family and friends surrounded her, helped her reclaim courage, the strength to fight again, and eventually scar tissue, strong but inflexible, began to grow.

She felt she could leave the Army, certain she had helped prove the effectiveness and essentiality of OT, confident the profession would now be a part of all civilian as well as military hospitals.

She accepted a position, again, as teacher. Dr. Bliss brokered the contract, a respite of a classroom in Bakersfield – committed parents, children eager to learn. He offered to negotiate a discharge from the military. There, she worked 3 days a week, returned to tennis, hiked in the mountains, and found time to think, ways to stretch the scar tissue and reconstruct her own spirit. She tried to paint but found it uninspiring. Her job was uninspiring too, undemanding, without challenge. She began to understand Paul's joy of life – clean silk sheets, warm showers and keyboards after weeks lying in blood and the stench of death. She had to find that place in herself that he loved, the fighter, find the strength to square her shoulder and push against the wall of life's inevitable horror. Little by little, she heard voices urging her to emerge from the trench. After a long and exhausting day on the trail where she was lost, wandering without direction, her father's words came to her as if spoken aloud: "Those who are strong must always look after the weak" and Paul's song began to play as if shoving her to feel again. The tune of "Rebel Angel", an unfinished concerto Paul had written about Ora, flashed through her mind over and over again. The piece had no ending, like her relationship with Paul, and her anguish escaped in deep sobs. At last, she felt she could see again, not the world of darkness she'd been floating in but the sky, ablaze with a full and glorious moon, and stars – real stars. She heard Doc Duncan's voice again, "Don't let 'em beat you, Orie".

This was a very fertile time in America, both intellectually and socially. The seeds had been sown in the 1830s by the transcendentalist movement, led by Henry David Thoreau and Ralph Waldo Emerson, both of Concord Massachusetts. A key tenet of transcendentalism is the inherent goodness of man and nature. And not just "man"; men _and women_ had divinely-inspired souls. Fast forward to the early 1920s, and these ideas had developed, become part of the culture, and spread. The women's rights movement definitely has roots in transcendental thinking. The author Louisa May Alcott, who was also an early feminist, lived in Concord from her childhood to her death, and was strongly influenced by Emerson. Her next-door neighbor was George Barton, who is widely regarded as the visionary founder of occupational therapy. Ora's unshakeable belief that the essential humanity of a man is undiminished by the loss of a limb clearly also flows from the transcendentalism stream of thought.

As Ora was recovering from her grief, she was reminded of Thoreau's words about the importance of living a purposeful life, and of Emerson's rallying cry: "God will not have his work done by cowards." That week, she received a letter from Eleanor Clarke Slagle, "The movement is losing impetus, and we've all got to get behind it and *push*." Another letter from Molly Wright stated: "We need you in this work, Ruggie. Don't forget, you helped to start it all." (Carlova & Ruggles, p. 113). Being needed was like a breath on the tiny ember of her spirit, causing it to glow and grow again. She was ready for her next challenge.

She returned to the military, but turned down the offer to head the new training program at Walter Reed General Hospital, as well as many other offers. Instead, she opted for starting a program at Pastime Park, a camp in the desert near Tucson, Arizona, for soldiers with tuberculosis. She had a chance to fight the disease that had claimed the man she loved. She heard Paul's words in her mind "You're an artist in people." Her strength began to return.

Pastime Park was a 13.5-acre parcel surrounded by eucalyptus trees. The park once housed a skating rink, bowling alley, dance hall, and tavern until it fell into disrepair. Ora arrived to find one brick building housing the boiler, two adobe buildings used as a ward and a kitchen, and 86 wood-frame cottages each 16 X 16 with 4-foot-tall wainscoting and mesh-screened windows. She saw windows covered with canvas flaps, roofs consisting of steel sheeting, and while all cottages were wired for electricity and included a single coal-burning stove, to say they were drab and depressing would be generous. This was the place for consumptives —over 275 veterans with tuberculosis. This place smelled of sand and lethargy; the men, who had once been soldiers, had devolved into insubstantial creatures waiting to die.

Ora had become quite skillful at helping to reconstruct men with *physical* disabilities. Working with TB patients was going to be a whole new challenge. These men suffered from lassitude, mentally, emotionally and physically – and had no sign of volition. Where once she had learned to see the man still present even though arms or legs were missing, now she had to find the humanity hidden behind a disease that turned men into ghostly creatures.

Photograph 32. Pastime Park tent cottages (top) and infirmary (bottom), circa 1920 (photographs courtesy of the Arizona Historical Society, Tucson).

     Ora was familiar with the task of struggling with the system to acquire resources. She had learned, from Paul, how to navigate the military system and find or create resources against all resistance. Her first task was to snoop around for supplies, as none of those she had requisitioned from the army had arrived. She found a storeroom of paint, and used it to paint the outside of a shack, her workshop. "A drab place like this depresses the spirit. My job is to lift up the spirit. I need a bright workshop," she announced to Dottie. "I don't intend to paint the shack myself, just watch," and reminded her of the story of Tom Sawyer's whitewash." (Carlova & Ruggles, p. 121). This was a common theme in Ora's story; there are many instances of environmental transformation, times she used ingenuity to transform environmental unsightliness to inspiring spaces that supported occupational engagement.

She started painting the shack a dazzling white, a magnet in the sun, and drew a crowd who brought with them a chorus of dry hacking coughs. Dull plops of spit landed in the cups they carried to catch their lungs' expulsion of poison. They were all flies in her trap. She wasn't doing it right, the men pointed out. Besides, an elegant young lady wearing impractical footwear and pearls shouldn't be painting a shack! Ora was prepared with buckets of scrapers and extra brushes. She refused their offers at first, saying they were too weak and frail by their own admission, but at last she yielded to their insistence, 'it's my turn now'. When the sun set on the third day, the shack was covered in 3 coats of white, and the interior was decorated in sunset red and evening mauve to capture the feel of the desert itself. Within two weeks, every tent base in the camp had been painted by the men who lived there, and signs put up to announce the space, Dew Drop Inn, Sunset Cottage, or The Last Gasp. Historical documents show the improved conditions, but no mention is made of the work, the Occupation, that reconstructed both the physical space and the men who grew well there. Eventually a model village grew from the collective effort with rock-lined lanes and reconstructed spirits.

After 3 years, Ora was told she was losing the spirit and beauty she had arrived with, becoming hardened by the place itself, exchanging that inner softness for riding skirts, boots and practical jackets, scar tissue overcoming all flesh. She could admit she had done her job at Pastime Park, establishing occupation as an intervention and an outcome, but time to move on had come. Ora requested a transfer back to Southern California, and was dispatched, assigned to begin the program at Santa Monica military sanatorium -- a job that would end in near-disaster (see poem "Court Martial").

After coming through her court martial with flying colors, Ora was transferred to the Soldiers' Home Military Hospital, in Sawtelle, CA, in 1924. After several years there, once again, she was overcome by the death of a patient, and decided to leave the army in 1927. She traveled to New York to meet with Eleanor Clarke Slagle, to tour the department at NY University and provide a report to AOTA. But once again, Ora perhaps had more vision than those who invited her were ready to see:

> "The training of some of the young people going into occupational therapy is deplorable. I spoke to girls who had no idea of *why* they were teaching patients certain occupations. It is not enough to be able to show a patient how to weave a basket or make a belt. The therapist must know *why* such activity will help the patient – or perhaps, more important, why certain activity will *not* help the patient.
>
> I believe the fundamental fault lies in our schools of occupational therapy. There are only a few of them but each seems to go pretty much its own way. There should be some system of general guidance, some method of accreditation. As it is now, anyone can start a school and turn out so-called occupational therapists."

The presentation was not well received. Ora and Eleanor had a falling out: Ora, practitioner was against prescriptive practice, wanted instead to preserve the art in the professional's hands, Eleanor felt equally strongly that the science of practice should govern (Carlova & Ruggles, p. 164). The clash deteriorated what had, to date, been a deep and mutually sustaining relationship and the two never spoke again.

Ora returned to San Fernando Valley to work in a psychiatric facility with Dr. William Bucher. She worked herself to a state of exhaustion and decided to travel to Hawaii (1929). She extended her trip by visiting Australia and New Zealand as well, working odd jobs to make enough money to survive on. When she finally returned to the states in 1931, after two years of wanderings, she opened an Art center of her own at the corner of Hoover and West Adams in LA, near the dorms of USC and began to take classes at the university.

In 1937, after six years of running the art center, Ora was invited to the Kula Sanatorium, in Maui, Hawaii, to start an OT program there. After four good years in Maui, she had a strong intuition it was time to return to the states again. She boarded a ship which, as it turned out, departed the day before the bombing of Pearl Harbor. Once established in the LA area again, working at Children's Hospital, Ora found herself appalled at the lack of **available** OTs for the inevitable need due to WW II. She took on training new Reconstruction Aide volunteers in the evenings, after her full time job at the Children's Hospital. The long days took their toll and at 50 years old, Ora collapsed (1945). In 1949 she again collapsed, this time with a burst appendix, and almost died (due to medical malpractice).

Poems from The Front

Poem for Oscar

> The Arizona Hut, a small organization led by Isabella Greenway at Pastime Park was a place at which crafts, made by patients, were sold to the public to raise money. - Kimmelman 1988.

> T.B. Kidder from the Advisory Service of the National Tuberculosis Association recommended that larger hospital-like institutions be designed to accommodate patients at different stages of recovery. -Kidder 1921

At last, all tents were whitewashed

Transformed from drab to invitation

Gleaming beacons of new potential.

Still, no supplies had arrived to entice men to engage

Until Oscar died, one nasty toad,

Horned, spiked but colorful

He'd been Al's companion scratched behind those invisible toad ears

He returned Al's kindness with cold-blooded love and affection

He'd been Ora's frequent fright

Scaring her when he jumped

Googly eyeing her when she moved about

Seducing her to the reptilian love he somehow engendered

Hidden prince, thespian.

Oscar obeyed clicks of the tongue, performed tricks even, played. He was beautiful

In his hideous hide, and beloved.

But he was part of a large and ever growing family

Of desert creatures. Prolific toads, lizards, vermin turned to lovable pets.

When Oscar died, Al stuffed him, used taxidermy skills to preserve his pet

Many would have found this ghoulish but Ora saw the curative occupation

And Al, who had just been waiting to die, took his new skill

Preservation, to other dead horned toads, and lizards, and assorted desert critters.

Oscar, friend in death and life, spirit guide one might say,

saved Al's life with cold-blooded death and resurrection. That toad

and others once stuffed, were sold throughout the Southwest

irresistible actors to tourists who wanted souvenirs of their arid travels.

Oscar and his kind found their way to museums, *Have you seen them?*

In France, London, even beyond. Others learned taxidermy

A new occupation, profitable, then they learned to stretch cacti into canvas

Paint blistering scenes of desert sunsets, make lamps from reptile skin.

And Al? he was discharged from Pastime Park, well enough at last

He started his own desert museum outside of Phoenix

Named it

Oscars.

The Beauty of the Ordinary

Ora foraged and found and offered weathered skulls and dusty rocks, sandstone that had been blasted by wind into a marbled palette; these became materials for curative art.

Ora could see beyond what was present to what might become

Saw the desert held many treasures -- rocks, semiprecious stones, sun-bleached skulls, flowering cacti.

Men who had only used muscles for gross skills – digging a trench, carrying guns, burying friends in battle or carrying them out

Used the desert's bounty to practice refined movement patterns of the hands,

tender precision turned craggy rock to precious gems which they wrapped and soldered into jewelry,

they carved ashtrays from wind-smoothed sandstone, and brushed watercolor across the carcasses of cacti.

These men, these materials, this place, this death-sentencing disease were

symbiotically reconstructed. The men soldered and wrapped their way to a new gainful employment, transforming the ordinary into extraordinary,

hideousness renovated into beauty

These Pastime men, ghost men, excavated exquisiteness before disregarded

in the desert's vermin, they longed, perhaps, and went searching for that hidden grace.

Once liberated from the Sanatorium, the rocks, the men both

weathered discards of mother nature became artisans, husbands, fathers

actors recast.

The importance of the ordinary

> "Nothing will sustain you more potently than the power to recognize in your humdrum routine, as perhaps it may be thought, the true poetry of life – the poetry of the commonplace, of the ordinary man, of the plain, toil-worn woman, with their loves and their joys, their sorrows and their griefs."– William Osler

Human tragedy and sorrow stand out

As will raw tenderness and beauty

The importance of the ordinary outlasts us all --

> A dying man who wanted to be moved into the path of sunlight

> A solider who passes while creating yet another extraordinary watercolor, his legacy documentation of the surprising yet familiar rippling of the desert's flatlands, now hanging in a museum.

> The conjured jewels from desert rock, invoked flowers from seed, and pet toads stuffed after years of loyal friendship.

Nothing sustains more than human humdrum

Nothing as important as the poetry of day to day routine, irrepressible cacophony of the commonplace

Ordinary man, the grasses from Nebraskan plains, Toilworn woman,

and grief that comes, then goes without mercy, the undulations of grief.

> *Aequanimitas,* imperturbability, eternal

---

* William Osler, from *The Student Life*, in *Aequanimitas*. * *Aequanimitas: With Other Addresses to Medical Students, Nurses and Practitioners of Medicine*. Second edition, with three additional addresses. Philadelphia: P. Blakiston's Son & Co., 1906.

<u>Nothing sustains me more potently than the poetry of the commonplace</u>

The true poetry of life

The patient weeping unceasingly

The strange beauty of sunlight as it slants across and stains weathered storefronts

The rough honesty of warriors, wounded, still whole still at war during sleep

The humdrum of routine as it soothes and repairs the spirit

The poetry of true life

The strange poetic quality when indomitable spirit shines through terminal disease

The joy of making a fool of oneself when fully engaged in pleasurable pursuit

The sorrow of human tragedy standing up and demanding to share the experience

The man imprisoned by the past struggling in the wrong direction to be free

The poetry of life true

Toilworn women artistically engraved with lines of love of joy of grief and barren harvests

Psychopathology helplessness phobic fears

The noiselessness of a tender gesture

The lack of any extraordinariness that is kindness blended to the fabric of life

The courage to be present to life when lived so fully

To true poetry

Court Martial

She was hated. Scorned. Mrs. High Society thought Ora

"Ridiculous". Who would think teaching grown men beadwork

Would be of use. Ora was said to be impertinent, an upstart

One who failed to know her place, a Nebraskan, after all.

This woman, a civilian who was placed in charge of what she failed to understand

A tyrant type to be sure, promised Ora

"I will have you broken, you you you insufferable troublemaker."

Patients tried to warn Ora

Told her to protect herself

To prepare for inevitable sabotage but Ora believed in her role

(Oh so naïve!) that great work would be sufficient armor.

Mrs. High Society had Ora arrested, removed from the facility, tried to shame her, wanting to expose this so-called visionary.

Funny how life turns and bends towards destiny. The court martial could not determine

Stymied by the question of status – occupational therapy civilian? Military? Or both?

It would drive the outcome, you see, dismissal, fired, or dishonorable discharge.

The court filled with veterans, some with no legs at all, some with empty sleeves,

The beaders, the weavers, the painters of walls, tree planters, even the one legged man who had learned to use gut to restring racquets for the tennis players at the officers club, the man who had just franchised his business. All there aiming to support Ruggie.

There they stood, a wall of the reconstructed, between Ora and ignorance. Ora was asked to defend herself and said:
"Your decision today will decide if I continue on as an Occupational Therapist but more you will influence the profession itself".

When the court spoke, at last, they

Dismissed the accuser in her spitting bluster. The officer read letters of Ora's past commendations into the record. They thanked her for her duties relative to rehabilitation, deemed her military after all. Ora was reassigned, her wages doubled, her new facility welcoming and well supplied.

And the tyrannical woman? She was dishonored, then fired.

Discharge

Shocked after leaving the army, 1927,

Ora found students of Occupational Therapy

In New York unable to say why an activity will help the patient

More

Why it would not.

She argued with Slagle

Argued that while anyone can start a school

Anyone can turn out so-called occupational therapists

To guide the work of the day to day doing of occupation

To assure those qualified to reach for the heart and the hands

to provoke outcomes of meaning and purpose

reconstructions that would break your heart over and over again

and let them break you over and over again

a life of precipice, abyss and spiritual creations

promote man to return unto himself

as man as father as driver as husband as student as lover as friend as squash player as musician as cook

this all took faith, not administration, art of innovation and not prescribed exactitudes of science

Slagle Administrator, not practitioner

The two locked in a life of festering disagreement

Ora Left

To be of use.

Breaking the bond between two great leaders

A decision she came to regret

Later.

Part IV: Winter: A Time of Reflection

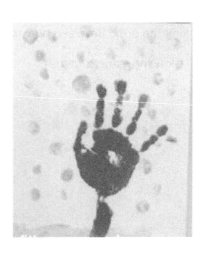

Ora Ruggles, born in 1894, was one of the most innovative occupational therapists in the profession's history. Still, few OTs today know her story.

1918-1920

Ora was trained as a teacher of manual arts. She arrived at Fort McPherson, Georgia in 1918 in response to the call for Reconstruction Aides during WWI. She faced resentment from both army personnel and nurses. She was inspired by the unfulfilled occupational needs of over 5000 veterans, wounded and left with few prospects of meaningful futures. She saw her calling there, to enable a man to return unto himself, and also give him a method with which to contribute to his family and community. Ora, raised with grit, gifted with beauty, and able to see beyond what was missing to see instead what still remained, helped these men reconstruct their spirits and their won humanity. She built futures for the men through basket weaving, music, educational tutoring (for those who had been to war but were unable to read), and other curative activity. The men learned rake knitting, happy to again use their hands and bodies to create. Only having access to reams of red yarn, their scarves – long and tasseled as the expression of their therapy – were sent home and worn lovingly by wives, mothers and girlfriends across the country, all red-scarfed women pride-fully carrying warm symbols of their loved ones recovering. Having experienced financial success as an artist entrepreneur herself, Ora facilitated the commerce of the soldier's art – an innovation of the era -- and in so doing, opened up viable means for employment and self-actualization. At her first post, Fort McPherson, she met Paul Remland, a former concert pianist who had lost 2 fingers from his right hand in the war. She and Paul were engaged, but he died before they could marry, in 1918, from tuberculosis (TB), a consequence of his shrapnel wounds. Ora was devastated, empty with grief. She left Fort McPherson with military commendations, having created a thriving highly regarded Occupational Therapy program.

1920-1923

After a short while at home in San Diego California, recovering from her grief, she reviewed several invitations from the army, including one to move back to the place her great grandfather had once lived, Bethesda MD, and start a training program at Walter Reed Army Hospital. Instead, she accepted another offer and moved to Tucson AZ where she would serve at Pastime Park's TB sanatorium. Perhaps she went there because TB had been the disease that had taken Paul away from her. Perhaps, as the place was known as 'where we go to die' she too felt lost and resigned to wither away. Here too she met with resistance, men who felt bothered by one who interrupted their only meaningful goal, 'waiting to die', men who were merely ghosts of human beings. She found a harsh desert, but also a new friend and mentor (Dottie). From the desert itself, she learned about the "poetry of the commonplace" and the "importance of the ordinary." Having few resources to work with, she raided the treasure of the desert – cacti, semi-precious stones, sunbaked skulls

– and used these materials to entice men to find a reason to get well and to live. The men carved lamps from the cacti, used taxidermy to preserve the dead but colorful lizards, geckos, horned toads. The works they produced were sold in the local shop Ora founded, then became treasures for tourists and made their way into museums and international art studios and galleries. TB, once something that lingered until one died from it, became something to live with. The soldiers moved outside of the Park, built homes, married, raised families, created communities, and the area grew and prospered. They were reconstructed through occupation. Ora created an OT program, trained her replacement and when the time came, she moved on in 1923.

During all these years, Ora, like many early Reconstruction Aides, communicated her discoveries, her successes and her struggles to William Rush Dunton, who curated what he received and published on the extraordinary evolution of a profession. Ora maintained a consistent and deliberate correspondence for more than three decades with Dr. Dunton, and also with Eleanor Clarke Slagle.

1923-1924

After leaving Pastime Park, Ora arrived at Santa Monica Sanatorium, hired to once again establish a program. By then, she was known as a remarkable innovator, a reliable pioneer and capable therapist of occupation. She was once again met with resistance, however, this time finding a uniquely horrible control freak as her supervisor. Referred to by the patients as Mrs. High Society (MHS), this woman, took an immediate dislike to Ora, found her a threat to the authority she felt she deserved. She said Ora was "insolent, insufferable, and a troublemaker." She set her sights on getting Ora *out*. Ora felt she would be protected if she just did a good job. MHS's ire was not reduced, instead, she told any who would listen about "this impertinent upstart who failed to understand her place, this nobody" and to Ora said directly, "I will see to it you are destroyed." MHS scoffed, "Imagine, doing beadwork with grown men – utterly ridiculous." Eventually Mrs. High Society had Ora *arrested*, removed from duty and ordered to appear before court martial. MHS, ironically, managed to benefit the profession of Occupational Therapy in a far reaching way. At the time, the roles of Reconstruction Aide and Occupational Therapist were unspecified by the army. The court was unable to determine if Ora was a member of the military or a civilian. Still, the court was aware of the deep appreciation the army had for the work of occupational therapy. The courtroom was filled by soldiers who came to profess the merit of Ora's intervention, the integrity of her character, and the value of her contribution. Letters of commendation, written by officers of great standing from Fort McPherson and Pastime Park were read into the record that day. What might have been a most unfortunate event instead resulted in the role of Occupational Therapist being declared as a class of military personnel, a profession in itself and one that contributed in undeniable ways. MHS was fired. Eleanor Clarke Slagle used the outcome of the trial to lobby for the passage of legislation recognizing the nascent profession's status in the healthcare field. This advocacy supported AOTA's efforts to create training programs.

1924-1927

Ora was reassigned to Soldier's Home in Sawtelle California, one of the largest military facilities in the United States at the time, given a generous raise and placed in charge of expanding a vibrant occupational therapy program. At Sawtelle, she was welcomed, greeted with ample resources, given a large well-equipped workshop, plenty of supplies and over a dozen therapists to work with and guide. Here, the veterans were from every war – Civil, Spanish-American, WWI. Some were very elderly. One elderly man drew Ora's attention with his silence. He sat, each day in full uniform, staring into seeming nothingness. After careful study with him and several quiet conversations, Ora discovered what he saw – he envisioned a garden, a Japanese garden to be precise, but he never imagined or hoped for its manifestation. He knew, believed, it would be his heart's work, and the army, he knew, was not known for its generous heart. Ora, however, saw it as clearly as he did, and more, saw the potential for occupation. The colonel, however, could not see how this was occupational therapy, the practice he had come to understand gave value through weaving and woodcraft. Ora appealed, "The theatrical aspect to Occupational Therapy is the opportunity for a project to catch man's imagination and show them they can create beauty with their own hands." Ora returned to share the news, the garden would be built, an occupational endeavor that would express the vision of this one man but provide therapeutic activity for many more. Ora, dubbed 'The Army's Heart,' set about co-creating the occupation of therapeutic gardening, the first of its kind. As this garden unfolded, the occupational outcomes increased – men found meaning in their work and meaning in their lives. The garden construction continued for years. Trees were planted, koi fish were released, pumps installed, small bridges added.

Ora learned more about occupational therapy, including that at times, there is only so much one can do, and she mourned the loss of a man who succumbed to alcoholism. She helped a former star tennis player find meaning in learning to expertly re-string racquets with gut and his own determination. Upon his release, he started a thriving racquet stringing business.

1927-1929

When Ora was discharged in 1927, her supervising officer said of her "she worked with unusual ingenuity." She was invited to visit New York by Eleanor Clarke Slagle, and tour the department at NY State, then to share her observations with AOTA at their meeting. Ora was not impressed with what she observed and advocated for a method of accreditation in occupational therapy education. She felt it was important to assure students graduate knowing how to select an occupation that is appropriate and just as importantly, how to recognize when an occupation is not of curative value to the patient. Ora advocated for OT to remain open to initiative and innovation while Eleanor wanted the profession to become aligned with the medical field. Both women were stubborn, the relationship unthreaded and Ora returned to civilian occupational therapy.

Taking her motivation and insights from what she had created in the military, Ora applied those insights to the private TB Sanatorium in San Fernando Valley referred to as Olive View. She used art as occupation, primarily, working to create opportunities for the residents. One woman, severely disabled from TB used a Bradford Frame. While the faint of heart might have seen hopelessness, Ora saw untapped potential. This woman and Ora worked together and created highly stylized clothing for dolls, shaped into ballerina and dancer poses that eventually earned the woman enough income to afford surgery that eased much of her restriction and allowed her to move out of the sanatorium and into a very successful dress making shop. Ora won over all her detractors in the private sector as she had done in the military, converting them into philanthropic champions of the arts and the disabled.

1929-1931

While she found her work satisfying, Ora yearned to travel, and in 1929, she and a friend decided to sell what they owned and travel the world. They worked along the way in hospitals and clinics, earning enough for the next leg of the journey. They traveled from Hawaii to New Zealand to Australia and more, until 1931 when they arrived back in the US to find the nation deep in a depression.

1931-1937

Ora worked as she could but times were indeed hard. The training program at Walter Reed was closed due to lack of funding. Only 5 schools remained open. Ora opted to make her own way, to use her ingenuity and a small inheritance to open an artist colony of her own. This was a rich and enjoyable time – Ora purchased a building in Casa Del Rosa, collected and nurtured artists in the business of their art, to build habits and routines of successful careers and internal fortitude. She built her own community, always having a pot of soup and bread warm and waiting to strengthen the spirits of the creative souls. She learned to architect wellbeing, became an alchemist of artistic spirits.

1937-1941

In 1937, she received an offer to come to Hawaii and create a program and she felt she could not resist. She stayed until 1941 when the time came to go home, she felt, and her friends on the island strongly encouraged an intuition to leave on December 5th, 1941. Two days later, while still at sea, Pearl Harbor was attacked by the Japanese, launching America into WWII. Ora and the other passengers on board found themselves zigzagging through the Pacific until finally arriving safely back in Los Angeles.

1941-1949

Her job was waiting, creating the program at California Children's Hospital. But also, the abysmal state of unpreparedness for the war was heavy on Ora, the lack of OTs ready to aid with the inevitable disabilities from war (only 3000 OTs were registered at the time). Ora taught a training program for Reconstruction Aides in the evenings and worked full time during the day. She said, once, she was a single woman with over 200 children.

Later years brought illness to Ora, her body hearty but not up to the challenge of her 12-hour, heart-breaking days of work. She had a burst appendix in 1949 and discovered the wonder drug, Penicillin, was a deadly allergen for her. She had moments of deep, debilitating despair in her life and was buoyed up again and again by her mentors, family and friends. She never married – saying many times that she was married to the full memory of Paul who even in death filled her heart and spirit with the moments they had shared. "We lived an entire lifetime together in the year we knew and loved one another in the flesh".

Later Years

In 1956, Ora turned 63 years old. At work, she found it increasingly hard to bear that so many of the children patients she worked with at the hospital ended up losing their battles. She put everything she had into their care, and often, that was not enough. Ora felt her own spirit draining away. Again, a friend restored her – reminding her of the power of occupation to heal, this time to heal and guide her own spirit and future self. Judy, a former student and now a leader in the World Federation of Occupational Therapy, provided Ora with the catalyst needed to create her own retirement. Ora moved to a small art community in Laguna Beach, purchased and rehabilitated a small bungalow, set up her easel on the beach, painted, foraged in the junk yard for materials to use in her crafts. She inspired, with her life, the lives of other artists and retirees. One of Ora's few regrets was not having reconnected with Eleanor Clarke Slagle and acknowledging that the move of OT to the medical field, as Eleanor had envisioned, was indeed an essential move for the profession. One has to wonder where Ora's place in the history of Occupational Therapy might have been had she maintained her relationship with one of the profession's most powerful visionaries.

The only available narrative of Ora's life ends with her retirement, being interviewed by the LA times and attending the national AOTA conference in 1960. When asked to reflect on her life and her 40-year career in occupational therapy, and offer some insight, Ora responded that what she had learned in her early years at Fort McPherson had remained the overarching truth of her life. "It's not enough to give a patient something to do with his hands. You must reach for the heart as well as the hands. It's the heart that really does the healing."

Ora attended conference in 1960. Her friend Judy shared about international Occupational Therapy. She listened to H. Dwyer Dundon speak about the potential role for Occupational Therapy in space travel. She was there when Claire Spackman, President of WFOT, spoke of the work Occupational Therapy was providing across the globe. She heard Helen Willard, President of AOTA, speak of the important and ever expanding presence of occupational therapists – now counting over 6000 registered OTs with the expectation of 1500 more within the next few years. She was in attendance for the annual Eleanor Clarke Slagle Lecture. Each year, before the current lecturer begins, the following year's lecturer is announced, and introduced on stage. In 1960, while Muriel Ellen Zimmerman waited to present her lecture on *Occupational Therapy Devices: Development and Direction* (and likely shared photographs of her invention, the Universal Cuff), the next Eleanor Clark Slagle Lecturer, Mary Reilly, would have been introduced. In 1961, Reilly would deliver one of the profession's most iconic lectures: *Occupational Therapy Can Be One of the Great Ideas of 20th-Century Medicine*, which included the precious quote, "Man, through the use of his hands, as they are energized by mind and will, can influence the state of his own health." One can speculate that perhaps Reilly was influenced by reading the 1957 article from the LA Times quoting Ora, who said the most important element of her life's work was learning that "It is not enough to give a patient something to do with his hands. You must reach for the heart as well as the hands. It's the heart that really does the healing."

Her friend, Judy McCall looked directly at her when she said, *Tragedy and suffering know no boundaries. If we fail those who experience these horrors, we fail those who suffer but we also fail ourselves. If we help, we fulfill our own life's purpose.* Ora was again asea, this time surely floating on the many ripples she had created and could witness by looking around her.

She returned to Santa Barbara where she died in 1971. She was 77 years old at that time.

Poems from Reflection and Retirement

Routine: All that remains

Only two of us attended his funeral

Me, his therapist, and Mildred, the nurse

His only possessions a broken jack-knife, one pencil stub, a soiled 2 cent stamp

His substance reduced to ash

Ready to be blown away with the slightest breath

The reaper inhales, takes him with her chilling fog.

I sold everything. I am leaving this place of death

My one way ticket will take me to New Zealand. Australia, Sydney, Hawaii.

I will learn to play bridge, dance, learn the words to today's popular songs,

    Button up your overcoat

    Makin' Whoopee

    Collegiate

    Show Me the Way to Go Home.

Old

Black

Void

Nothingness

Shadow. Isolation.

Enemy of time.

Strangling hope day after day after day

Depression, gravity bearing down

Emotional paralysis.

No juice for life or creating.

I wither

Dry, waiting, asea

I am old now. Lost

All I see are those who are old like me

Lost, alone, waiting.

Gloom, manifest in age-spotted faces

Phantasmal. Insolent silence engulfs sound

I am not living,

I am merely waiting to die.

Role

Day upon day

No one needing me

nothing undone

No one needing to be seen for treatment

No need pulling on me to resolve

I am without engagement for my hands

My heart has no one reaching for it

I am alone

But more

Lonely.

My life once spent

Day upon day

Exhausted mucking out the stench of war

To touch the light beneath

I am lost, now, in time

Strangled by too much time.

Without the constant demands from others

To organize my day

I am lost

No role

No need

Who am I?

Habitual

I'd like to say you get used to being around the dying

but you never do

It rips a hole each time, like the oyster, a grain of sand

Soothed by many baths of salt, covered, opalescent but when removed

An irreplaceable wound.

But scars are a testament to life, like the indentation left where once a pearl rested

Evidence that you have loved deeply, deeply enough to be cut, chiseled, tooled.

Scar tissue is stronger than flesh ever, ugly to those who do not understand the beauty of a fighter willing to fight again.

I loved one man, and lived a full life of being loved in the one year we lived

Together.

But it is grief that erodes us, and it comes unbidden, unexpected, heavy and in undulating waves. At first all I could do was float, grab onto something strong and buoyant. The habit of living overtakes a person,

Breathe, float, breathe. I don't know what else to do. My limbs ache, my only thought is to resist drowning.

But even waves lose interest and move on, come less often

I find the rogue waves to be the most malicious, unanticipated,

They rise up in the calmest of moments,

huge merciless hands reaching out and pushing my head under again

at Christmas,

when I hear the keys of a piano in a bar, tickled by fingers I wish could touch me again after they fold carefully in a lap I love.

I am never prepared for the viciousness of grief, at times I have surrendered,

I would sink into the quiet nothingness of dark undertow,

at times I touched the bottom, found ground, and rose up but mostly, I have to confess, I was pulled, grabbed by another who saw me surrender to the water,

a hand would reach into the murky darkness, grab me by the collar and pull me to the surface, to shore, soaking wet, sputtering.

It wasn't will but habit that had me hang on to that small ember inside me that resisted total surrender.

Take it from me, Ora, I would hear Paul whisper the waves don't stop, the storms the wreckage the waves but you will survive, you must survive, you have to hold on to knowing there is breath to fight for, there is light to swim toward and you'll make it if you have to crawl– and if you are lucky, you will have lots of scars from lots of loves and losses. Life is nothing but joy lived in-between pile after pile of devastation, death waiting while you enjoy silk underwear, long hot baths, piano keys that sing halleluiah even when tickled by only eight.

At this moment
It is truth
To pray over yeast
Expanded.

After kneading the dough
In strong loving patterns
Folded and refolded upon itself until
A sticky coagulant
Is rendered, silken.

This house warmed
The oven primed
Bread tucked in
Pan centered on heated rack
I smooth the finish and

Pause.

Yes, this is right
To pray at this door
Just as my mother prayed
And hers before her.

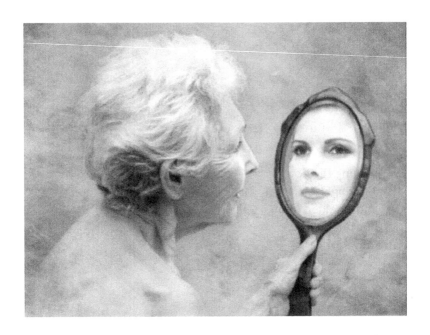

AOTA Centennial Vision

We envision that occupational therapy is a powerful, widely recognized, science-driven, evidence-based profession with a globally connected and diverse workforce meeting society's occupational needs.

AOTA vision 2025 to guide the profession beyond 2017

Occupational therapy maximizes health, well-being, and quality of life for all people, populations, and communities through effective solutions that facilitate participation in everyday living.

References

Alcott, L.M. and Alcott, M. (2008). Little Women Abroad: The Alcott Sisters Letters from Europe (1870-1871) D. Shealy, (Ed.). Athens, GA: University of Georgia Press.

Barton, G. E. (n.d.). Editorial. Archives of occupational therapy. Vol II No 5. Available at http://otsearch.aota.org/files/archives/vol2/VOL2_409-410.pdf

Byerly, C. R. (2014). Camp Follower: Tuberculosis in World War II in *Good Tuberculosis Men: The Army Medical Department's Struggle with Tuberculosis.* Retrieved March 1, 2017 from http://www.cs.amedd.army.mil/FileDownloadpublic.aspx?docid=5c14d2f0-eeb7-47e6-bde0-98ac850ecbd6. Department of the Army.

Carlova. J. & Ruggles, O. (1961) The healing heart. New York: Julian Messner

Gutman, S.A. (1994). Influence of the U.S. military and occupational therapy Reconstruction Aides in World War I on the development of occupational therapy. *American Journal of Occupational Therapy* 49(3), 256-262.

Peloquin, S. M. (2005). The 2005 Eleanor Clarke Slagle Lecture—Embracing our ethos, reclaiming our heart. *American Journal of Occupational Therapy*, 59, 611–625.

Peloquin, S.M. (1990). The Patient-Therapist Relationship in Occupational Therapy: Understanding Visions and Images. *American Journal of Occupational Therapy* 44(1), 13-21.

Peloquin, S.M. (1991). Occupational therapy service: Individual and collective understandings of the founders, Part 2. *American Journal of Occupational Therapy* 45(8), 733-744.

Peloquin, S.M. (1991). Occupational Therapy Service: Individual and Collective Understandings of the Founders, Part 1. *American Journal of Occupational Therapy* 45(4), 352-360.

Tucson Health Seekers: Design, Planning and Architecture in Tucson for the Treatment of Tuberculosis Retrieved March 1, 2017 from https://preservetucson.org/sites/default/files/project-doc/TucsonHealthSeekersMPDFtext_AZ_PimaCounty.pdf. Tucson Historical Preservation Foundation.

Made in the USA
Middletown, DE
27 May 2019